Sculpture

Sue Nicholson

QEB Publishing, Inc.

Published in the United States by
QEB Publishing, Inc.
23062 La Cadena Drive
Laguna Hills, CA 92653

www.qeb-publishing.com

Library of Congress Control Number: 2005921167

ISBN 1-59566-085-2

Written by Sue Nicholson
Designed by Susi Martin
Photographer Michael Wicks
Editor Paul Manning

Publisher Steve Evans
Creative Director Louise Morley
Editorial Manager Jean Coppendale

The author and publisher would like to thank:
Billy and Dylan
Sarah Morley for making the models
Ella Slater for the sculptures and Sue Nicholson for
the photographs on pages 6–7

Printed and bound in China

Note to teachers and parents

The projects in this book are aimed at children in
grades 1–3 and are presented in order of difficulty,
from easy to more challenging. Each can be used as
an independent activity, or as part of another subject.

The ideas in the book are offered as inspiration, but
children should always be encouraged to work from
their own imagination and first-hand observations.

All projects in this book require adult supervision.

Sourcing ideas
★ Encourage the children to source ideas from their
   own experiences as well as from books,
   magazines, the Internet, art galleries, or museums.
★ Ask them to talk about different types of art they
   have seen at home, on field trips, or on vacation.
★ Use the "Click for Art!" boxes as a starting point
   for finding useful material on the Internet.*

★ Suggest that each child keeps a sketchbook
   of his or her ideas.

Evaluating work
★ Encourage the children to share their work and talk
   about their ideas and ways of working. What do
   they like best/least about it? If they did it over, what
   would they do differently?
★ Help children judge the originality of their work and
   appreciate the different qualities in others' work.
   This will help them value ways of working that are
   different from their own.
★ Encourage the children by displaying their work.

* Website information is correct at the time of going to
   press. However, the publishers cannot accept liability
   for information or links found on third-party websites.

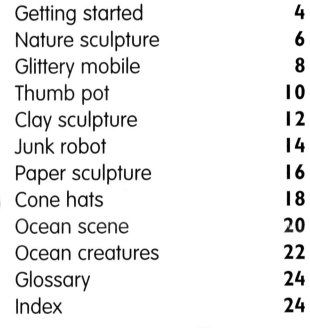

Contents

Words in bold, **like this**, are explained in the Glossary on page 24.

Getting started

A sculpture is a **three-dimensional (3D)** model. This book shows you how to make different kinds of sculpture, from a **clay** pot to a glittery hanging mobile. Here are some of the things you need to get started.

Top tip

Always ask first before you use something to make a sculpture!

Basic equipment

- Safety scissors
- Adhesive tape
- Felt-tip pens
- Pencils and ruler
- Poster/acrylic paints and brushes
- **craft glue**

You will also need some extra things listed for each project.

Paper

For many of the models you will need white paper, card stock, poster board, or cardboard. You may also like to use:

- colored paper
- tissue paper
- **construction paper**

4

Cardboard

Start a collection of cardboard boxes to use in your sculptures. Look for:

- cereal boxes
- toilet paper or paper towel tubes
- large grocery boxes
- cardboard egg cartons

Craft materials

Keep a box of things with an interesting **texture** or shape to decorate your sculptures. For example:

- ★ Shells, dried beans, and seeds
- ★ String, yarn, ribbon, and embroidery thread
- ★ Sequins, buttons, and beads
- ★ Nails, screws, paperclips, and washers
- ★ Foil and bottle tops

Nature sculpture

Have fun making outdoor sculptures from smooth stones, fallen flowers and leaves, twigs, moss, or feathers. You can find all the things you need for free in parks, woods, fields, or your own yard!

Sculpture ideas

Natural materials can make great outdoor sculptures. Here are some ideas to start you off:

★ Arrange berries in a pattern on moss.

★ Overlap fallen leaves in the shape of a circle or a star.

★ Arrange flower petals on a stone or rock.

★ Make rows of pebbles or shells on the beach.

★ If it's been snowing, make a sculpture out of snow.

★ If it's been raining, trace lines in mud with a sharp stone or twig, then add a **pattern** of fallen leaves.

A spiral of tiny pebbles on a flat stone

Changing nature

Ask a grown-up to photograph your nature sculpture. Go back to it the next day and take another photograph to show how it has been changed by wind, rain, or animals.

Click for Art! To see nature sculptures by Andy Goldsworthy, go to **http://ea.pomona.edu/goldsworthyart.html** For more images, click on "Gallery." Click on a photo for a closer look.

Colorful petals and leaves on grass

Shells arranged in the shape of a star

7

Glittery mobile

A mobile is a sculpture that moves. This glittery hanging mobile is fun to watch as it gently twists and spins.

1 Ask an adult to help you cut two pieces of dowel, about 12 in (30 cm) long.

You will need:

- Two lengths of dowel stick
- Cellophane or food wrap
- A thick knitting needle
- String or transparent nylon line
- Glitter

Top tip

To add sound to your sparkly mobile, attach tiny bells to the end of some of the glitter curls.

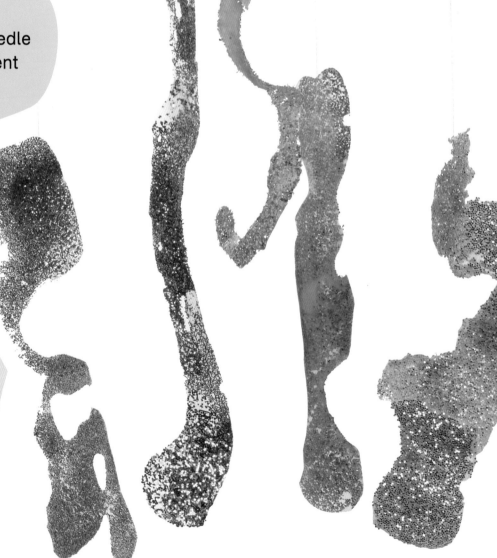

2 Arrange the two pieces of dowel in a cross shape and tie them together at the center with string.

3 Spread out a sheet of cellophane on a flat surface. Tape it down at each corner.

4 Squeeze out some glue, then use a strip of cardboard to shape it into thick blobs with long swirling tails.

5 Sprinkle different-colored glitter on the glue, then let it dry.

6 Carefully peel the glitter curls from the cellophane. Make a small hole in the top of each one with a thick knitting needle.

7 Tie the glitter curls onto the dowel with string or transparent nylon line. Hang up the mobile and watch it twist and twirl!

Click for Art!

To see an interactive virtual mobile, go to **www.nga.gov/kids/zone/zone.htm** and click on "Mobile."

Thumb pot

This project shows you how to make a simple clay pot and decorate it with lively colors and patterns.

Add simple shapes like this star to decorate your pot.

1 Roll the clay into a ball between the palms of your hands. It should be about half the size of a tennis ball.

2 Holding the ball in one hand, push the thumb of your other hand into the middle of the clay.

3 Open out the middle of the pot by gently pinching the sides between your thumb and fingers. Keep turning the pot as you pinch, to keep the sides the same thickness.

4 When you like the pot's shape, flatten the bottom by tapping it gently on a flat surface. Let it dry out a little, then decorate it using modeling tools, or by adding pieces of clay.

Click for Art!

To see examples of clay pottery, go to **www.thebritishmuseum.ac.uk/compass/** and search for "clay pot."

Decorating your pot

When your clay pot is almost dry, decorate it with a **relief pattern** or press patterns into the side with modeling tools. If you don't have special pottery tools, use:

★ the tip of a pen or pencil
★ a large nail
★ the end of a ruler
★ a blunt metal knife or fork

5 When the clay is completely hard, paint your pot with poster paint and let it dry. Finish it off with a coat of craft glue mixed with a little water.

"Studs" made from flattened balls of clay

Long thin snakes of clay stuck on with a little water

Clay sculpture

People have been making clay models for thousands of years. For this project, you can use self-hardening modeling clay, so you don't need to fire it in a **kiln**.

You will need:
- Self-hardening modeling clay
- Modeling tools

1 Tear off a piece of clay and work it into the shape of a head with your fingers.

2 Add features by sticking on extra pieces of clay or cutting away areas with a modeling tool. Make hair by squeezing clay through a garlic press so it comes out in long strands.

3 Stop when you're happy with how your model looks, and let the clay harden.

Top tip

Coat your finished model with glue mixed with a little water. The glue looks white at first, but dries to a clear, shiny finish.

4 Paint your model with poster paints and let it dry.

Click for Art!

To see sculptures by Henry Moore, go to **www.henry-moore-fdn.co.uk/** Click on the link to "Perry Green," then on the interactive map, then on photos of sculptures.

Animal shapes

Here are some simple animal shapes made out of clay:

Junk robot

You can make fantastic sculptures out of scrap materials! This robot has been made from cardboard boxes and tubes spraypainted silver.

You will need:
- A large cardboard box
- Smaller boxes for the robot's lower body, hands, and feet
- 9–10 toilet paper tubes
- **Corrugated** cardboard
- Silver spraypaint

1 Glue down the open top of a cardboard box. Ask an adult to help you make a hole in the top and push in a toilet paper tube for the robot's neck. Secure it with adhesive tape.

2 Glue on a smaller cardboard box to make the lower part of the robot's body. Make two holes underneath and attach toilet paper tubes for the legs.

3 Tape two toilet paper tubes together to make each of the robot's arms. Secure them to the sides of the robot's body with craft glue.

Click for Art! To see Picasso's "Head of a Bull," a sculpture made with a bicycle seat and handlebars, go to **www.artviews.org/cosby.htm** and scroll down.

Top tip
For a shiny, metallic look, ask an adult to help you spraypaint your robot silver.

14

4 Cut out ears, eyes, and a mouth from cardboard and glue them to a small cardboard box to make the robot's head.

5 Ask an adult to help you cut a hole in the bottom of the head and attach it to the robot's neck.

6 Glue on feet made from small cardboard boxes. Paint the robot when the glue is dry.

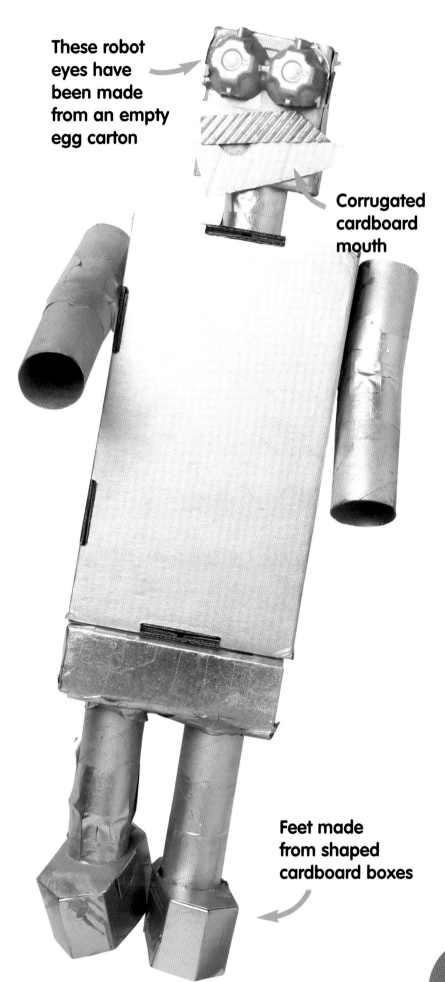

These robot eyes have been made from an empty egg carton

Corrugated cardboard mouth

Feet made from shaped cardboard boxes

Paper sculpture

This colorful bird has been made out of different kinds of paper that have been folded, creased, or curled to look three-dimensional.

Bird of paradise

You will need:
- Colored construction paper
- Scrunched-up newspaper
- Ribbon or yarn
- A stapler

1 Ask an adult to help you copy and enlarge the bird shape below onto two sheets of brightly colored paper.

2 Cut out one of the shapes and crease it with a ballpoint pen top, roughly following the dotted line. Do this several times until you can fold the paper so it bulges in the middle.

3 Do the same with the other shape, but crease it on the opposite side.

4 Ask an adult to help you staple the two pieces of paper together so the sides bulge out. Leave a gap at the bird's head and tail, then stuff it with scrunched-up pieces of newspaper.

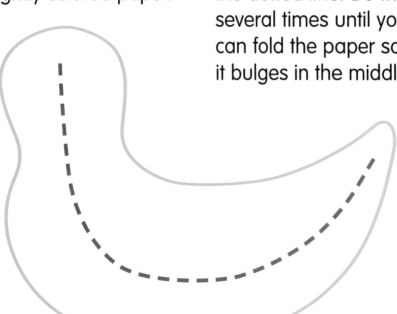

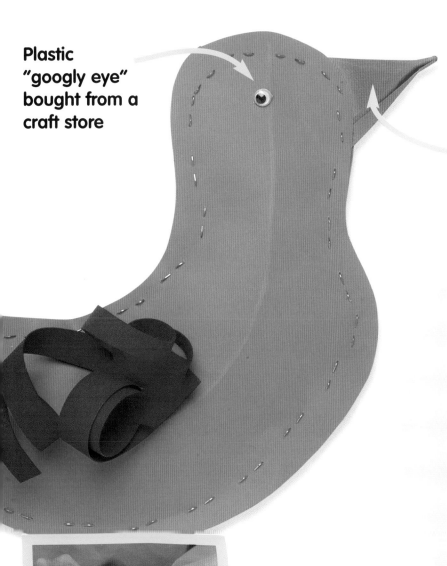

Plastic "googly eye" bought from a craft store

Paper beak folded and glued in a cone shape

paper decorations

1 Cut out 6–10 strips of paper about 1 in (3 cm) wide.

2 Leave two strips 12 in (30 cm) long. Cut two strips 11 in (28 cm) long, and cut two more strips 10 in (26 cm) long.

6 Glue long brightly colored paper curls to make the bird's tail, and shorter curls for the wings.

3 Arrange the strips with the long ones on the outside and the shorter ones in the middle.

5 Using safety scissors, cut out thin strips of colored paper and wind them tightly around a pen or pencil so they curl.

7 Hang the finished sculpture on the wall with a length of ribbon or yarn.

4 Staple the strips together at the top and bottom, so the shape balloons out, then hang it up.

17

Cone hats

These cute hats are great to make—and fun to wear!

1 Ask an adult to help you draw a big circle on a sheet of cardboard and cut it out with safety scissors. Cut a straight line from the edge of the circle to the exact center.

2 Overlap the edges to make a cone shape that fits your head, then secure the edges together with glue or tape.

3 Paint your hat and decorate it with ribbons, sequins, or glitter.

4 Ask an adult to help you make a hole in each side of the hat. Cut a piece of elastic or ribbon and tie it through the holes.

You will need:
- A large sheet of cardboard
- Ribbons, sequins, stick-on gems, glitter, and feathers for decoration
- A length of elastic or ribbon

Click for Art!

To see sculptural hats designed by Pip Hackett, go to **www.vam.ac.uk/collections/fashion/** and search for "Pip Hackett."

Wizard's hat

Moons and stars cut from foil

Animal ears

1 Using safety scissors, cut out a strip of cardboard 2 in (5 cm) wide and long enough to go around your head plus an extra 1 in (2 cm).

2 Fit the strip around your head, and then ask an adult to staple the ends of the cardboard together.

3 Cut out animal ear shapes from cardboard and glue them to the band.

Rabbit ears painted with poster paints

Top tip

Try cutting out different sizes of circles. The bigger the circle, the wider or taller the hat. The wizard's hat was made from a circle measuring 39 in (1 m) wide.

19

Ocean scene

First make and decorate this box for a 3D ocean scene—then turn the page to find out how to fill it with fish and other sea creatures!

1 Cut off the flaps on the open side of the box, or fold them back and glue them to the sides.

You will need:

- A large cardboard box
- Blue cellophane
- Newspaper
- Sandpaper, pebbles, and shells

2 Ask an adult to help you cut a rectangular hole in the top of the box to let in light at the back. Paint the box blue inside and out.

3 Glue a piece of blue cellophane underneath the hole in the top of the box to create a watery blue light.

4 Glue sandpaper, small pebbles, and shells onto the bottom of your box to make a sandy seabed.

Click for Art!

To discover the outdoor sculptures of Oldenburg and van Bruggen:
www.metmuseum.org/explore/oldenburg/artist.html

5 Scrunch up some old newspaper and pack it tightly into a corner of your box. Secure it in place with tape and glue.

6 Tear more newspaper into strips and glue 2–3 layers over the scrunched-up newspaper, overlapping them as you go.

7 When the glue is dry, paint the newspaper brown or gray, for rocks.

Now turn the page to find out how to make the sea creatures to put in the box.

Ocean creatures

Now that you've made the box for your 3D ocean scene, it's time to fill it with colorful fish and sea creatures.

You will need:
- Self-hardening modeling clay
- A plastic bottle
- Glitter glue
- A clear plastic food bag
- Tissue paper
- Transparent nylon line

Clay crab and fishes

Use self-hardening clay to make these sea creatures for your ocean scene.

Have fun decorating your models with bright colors and spotted patterns!

Plastic bottle fish

These fish were cut out of a large plastic bottle, then painted with wavy and zigzag patterns.

Ask an adult to make a hole at the top of your fish, so you can hang it from the top of your box with transparent nylon line.

plastic bag jellyfish

This sea snail was made from colored self-hardening clay

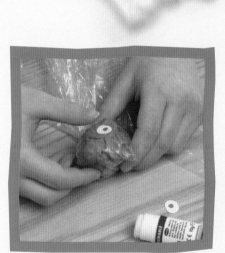

1 Push some colorful scrunched-up tissue paper into a clear plastic food bag.

This seahorse was made from cardboard, built up with layers of glued newspaper strips, and then painted

2 Tie the bag around the middle, then cut the open end into strips for the jellyfish's tentacles.

3 Glue on some big cardboard eyes or some "googly eyes" from a craft store.

Click for Art!

To design a 3D shape on an interactive art site, go to **www.nga.gov/kids/zone/zone.htm** and click on "3D Twirler." You may have to download a program to work it.

Glossary

clay type of stretchy, sticky earth used to make pots

construction paper thick, textured paper often used in scrapbooks

corrugated type of cardboard shaped into folds with a pattern of ridges and grooves

craft glue strong white glue; can be mixed with water and painted on a model to make it shine

kiln large, hot oven used to fire clay to make it last (self-hardening clay doesn't need to be fired in a kiln)

modeling tool special tool made of shaped wood or metal used to sculpt or make patterns in clay

pattern the repetition of shape, line, or color in a design

relief pattern when part of a pattern sticks out from a background

texture the surface or "feel" of something; for example, rough, soft, furry, bumpy, smooth, or velvety

three-dimensional (**3D**) when something has height, width, and depth, instead of just being flat

Index